Forever Grateful To You:

Made in the USA
Las Vegas, NV
25 November 2022

60206151R00066